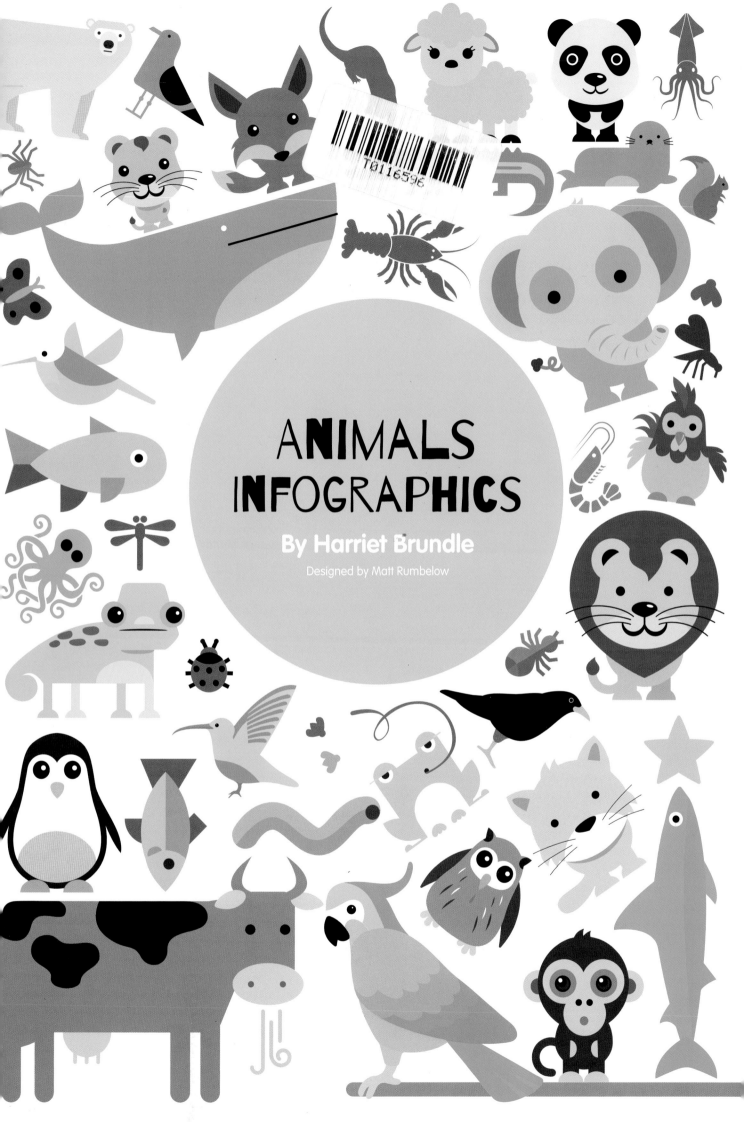

ANIMALS INFOGRAPHICS

By Harriet Brundle

Designed by Matt Rumbelow

BookLife
PUBLISHING

©BookLife Publishing 2019

Distributed by:
Independent Publishers Group
814 N. Franklin Street
Chicago, IL 60610

ISBN: 978-1-78637-630-5

Written by:
Harriet Brundle

Edited by:
Grace Jones

Designed by:
Matt Rumbelow

ANIMALS
Infographics

Contents

Words that are <u>underlined</u> are explained in the glossary on page 31.

Animals

An animal is a living <u>organism</u>. All animals are divided into groups based on their characteristics. This is called classification.

Kingdom – All living organisms belong to one of five kingdoms, they are the animal, plant, fungi, bacteria and <u>protist</u> kingdoms.

Animals   Plants   Fungi   Bacteria   Protist

Vertebrate

Invertebrate

Phylum – The grouping of organisms based on sharing similar body characteristics, for example if they are <u>vertebrates</u> or <u>invertebrates</u>.

Class – Organisms are divided into smaller groups, called classes, that share further similar characteristics. For example, classes of vertebrate animals are mammals, birds, fish, reptiles and amphibians.

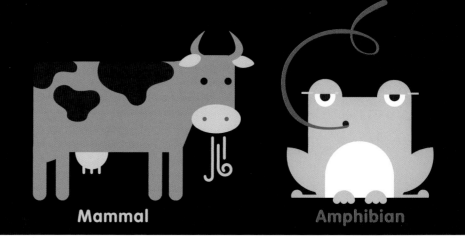

Mammal   Amphibian

Order – The order of an organism mostly depends on what type of food it eats. For example, a mammal that eats meat belongs to the carnivorous order.

Carnivore

Herbivore

Tiger

Lion

Family – Species that share similar physical characteristics, such as cats, which have long tails and strong jaw muscles. Lions and tigers belong to the family of cats known as *felidae*.

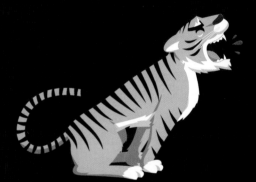

Genus – Certain species that share further characteristics with one another. For example, species from the cat (felidae) family that can roar belong to the *panthera* genus.

Species – A group of living things that share more distinctive characteristics and are able to reproduce with each other.

No two tigers have the same stripe pattern.

Siberian Tiger

Kingdom:	Animalia
Phylum:	Chordata
Class:	Mammalia
Order:	Carnivora
Family:	Felidae (cat)
Genus:	Panthera tigris
Species:	Panthera tigris altaicia

Mammals

A mammal is a class of animal that breathes air through lungs, has a backbone and grows hair. Most mammals give birth to live young. All female mammals have mammary glands, which are <u>organs</u> that produce milk to feed their young. Humans are also mammals.

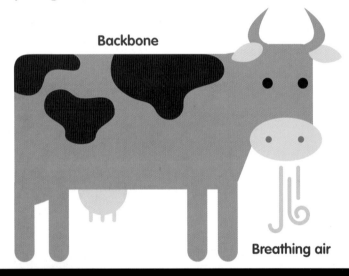

Backbone

Breathing air

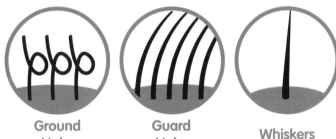

Ground Hairs	Guard Hairs	Whiskers

Many mammals grow more than one type of hair on their bodies. Ground hairs are short and thick to help maintain body temperature. Guard hairs are longer and protect the animal from moisture. Whiskers are stiff hairs that help an animal to feel their way around.

Mammals are warm-blooded animals, which means that they maintain a stable body temperature, even if it's very hot or very cold in their habitats.

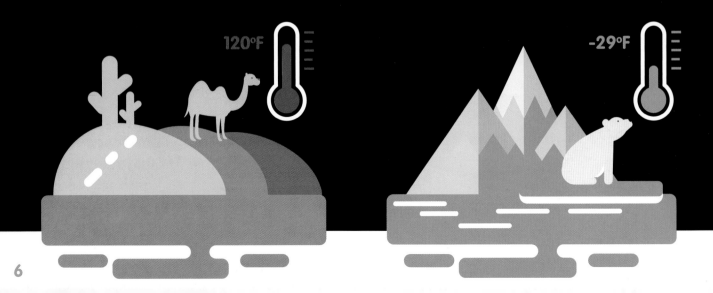

120°F

-29°F

The largest mammal on Earth is the blue whale at 100 feet long.

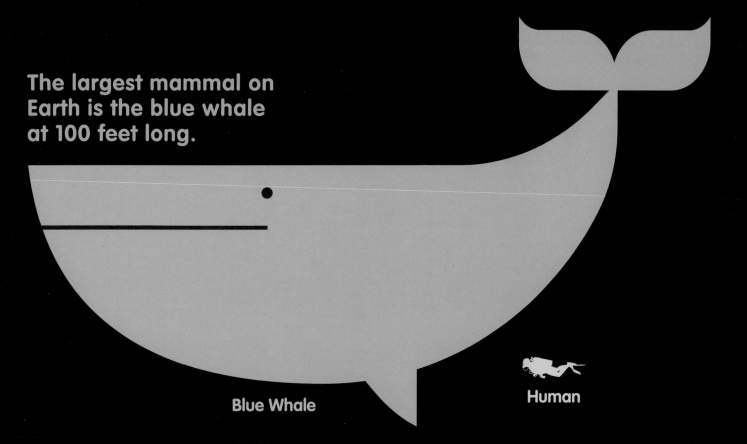

Blue Whale

Human

Etruscan Shrew

Human Hand

The Etruscan shrew is the smallest mammal on Earth at under two inches long.

It is thought there are around 5,000 different species of mammal. Over 2,000 mammal species are rodents such as rats and mice.

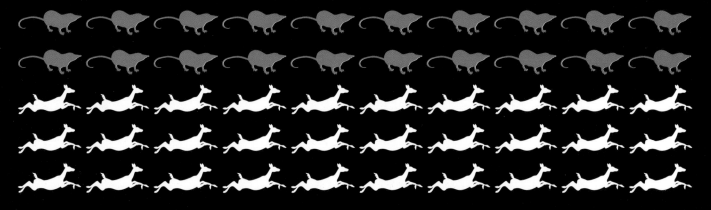

Birds

Birds are a class of animal that are warm-blooded, have a backbone, feathers and hard beaks without teeth. All birds have two wings; however, not all can fly. Birds also lay hard-shelled eggs.

A bird's beak is usually shaped according to what it eats.

Beak used for cracking seeds

Beak used for picking up insects

Beak found on birds of prey that need to catch live food

Fossil records show that birds are the last surviving dinosaurs.

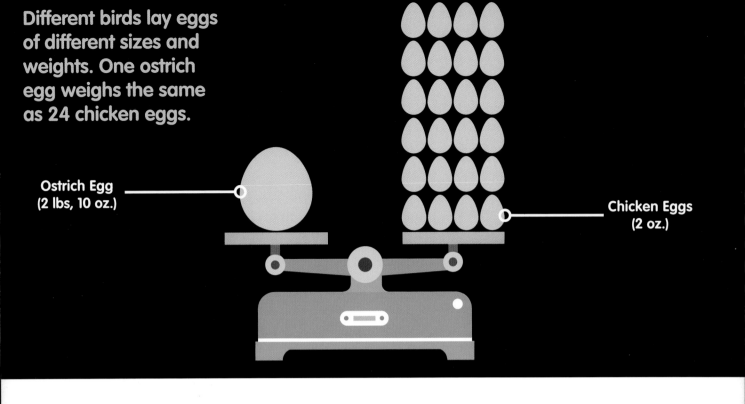

Different birds lay eggs of different sizes and weights. One ostrich egg weighs the same as 24 chicken eggs.

Ostrich Egg
(2 lbs, 10 oz.)

Chicken Eggs
(2 oz.)

Feathers help to keep a bird warm, protect it from moisture and <u>camouflage</u> it.

Reptiles

Reptiles are a class of animal that have backbones, skin covered in scales, and (mostly) lay soft-shelled eggs on land. Reptiles are air-breathing animals and many live on land or in water.

Reptile Eggs

There are four main reptile groups: turtles and tortoises, lizards and snakes, crocodiles and alligators, and the <u>tuatara</u>.

Tortoise

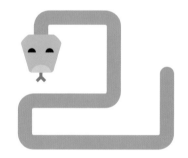

Snake

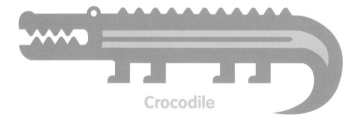

Crocodile

Tuatara

175

One tortoise, called Harriet, lived to be around 175 years old!

Reptile scales protect the animal and help it to keep moisture in its body so that it does not <u>dehydrate</u>. There are two types of scales.

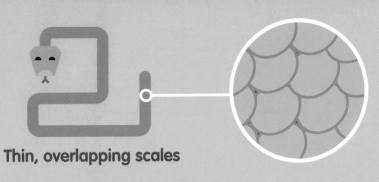

Thin, overlapping scales

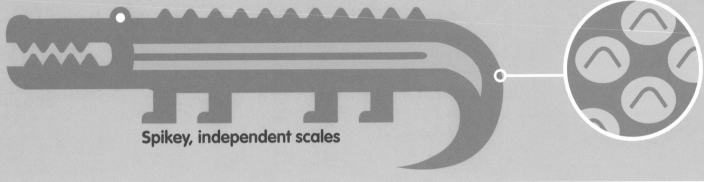

Spikey, independent scales

Reptiles are cold-blooded animals. This means that a reptile's body temperature is not stable and will change depending on the temperature of its environment.

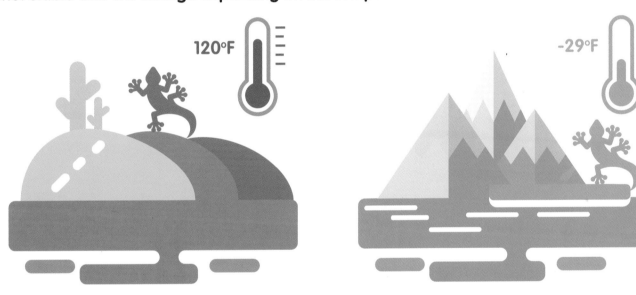

120°F

-29°F

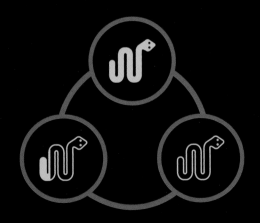

Reptiles regularly shed their scales. Some reptiles, like snakes, shed their whole outer skin in one piece, which is then replaced with a new one underneath.

Reptiles inhabit every continent of the world, except Antarctica.

Amphibians

Amphibians are cold-blooded animals that have a backbone. There are more than 6,000 species of amphibians.

When they are first born, amphibians live in water and have <u>gills</u>. As they grow, they develop lungs to breathe air on land.

Frog

Life Cycle of a Frog

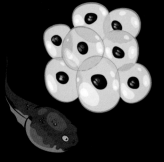

Frogs have already developed gills and a tail before they hatch. They use their tail to wriggle out of their egg. At this stage in their lives, frogs are called tadpoles.

The tadpole begins to grow two back legs and the tail becomes shorter.

The tadpole grows two front legs and begins to develop lungs in order to come up to the top of the water and breathe air.

The froglet can now live both on land and in water. Once it loses the rest of its tail it will become a fully grown adult frog.

Many amphibians have long, sticky tongues that help catch their prey.

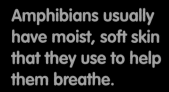

Amphibians usually have moist, soft skin that they use to help them breathe.

They also lose moisture through their skin, so they tend to live nearer to water in order to replenish the water in their bodies and keep their skin moist.

Amphibians are threatened by extinction because of habitat loss, pollution and disease.

The smallest amphibian is a species of frog that is 0.27in long!

Actual size

Fish

Fish are animals that have gills and a backbone, are cold-blooded and do not have limbs with <u>digits</u>. Most fish are covered in scales and must live in water to survive.

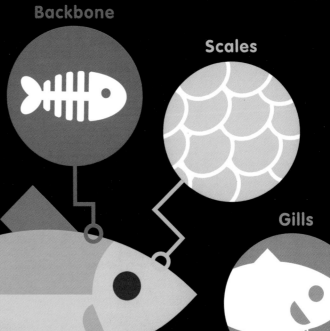

Backbone

Scales

Gills

There are three main types of fish:

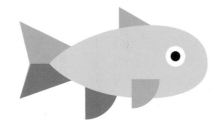

Jawless fish are fish with no jaws.

Bony fish have skeletons made from bone.

Cartilaginous fish have skeletons made from <u>cartilage</u>.

Sailfish can swim at speeds of up to 68 mph!

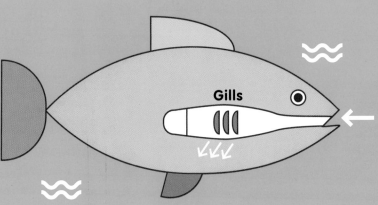

Gills

Fish use their gills to breathe. As water passes over tiny <u>blood vessels</u> in the gills, oxygen enters the fish's body.

Many species of fish have a swim bladder, which is a special air-filled organ that helps them to stay afloat. Cartilaginous fish do not have a swim bladder and so they must keep swimming all the time.

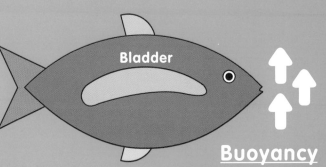

Bladder

<u>Buoyancy</u>

There are 32,000 different species of fish.

Vertebrates

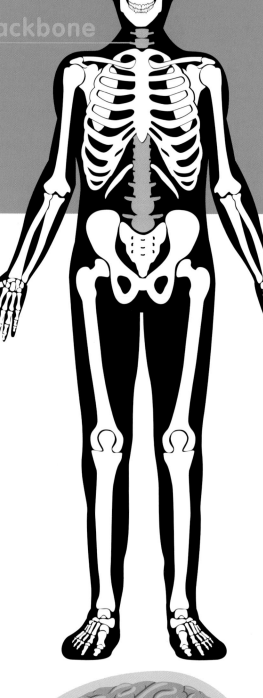

Vertebrates are any species of animal with a backbone and a skeleton. One of the jobs of the backbone is to protect the spinal cord, which connects all the different parts of the body to the brain.

Mammals, birds, reptiles, fish and amphibians are all vertebrates.

Vertebrates have a well-developed brain and skeleton and tend to be more intelligent than invertebrates.

Simple brain

Invertebrate

Vertebrate

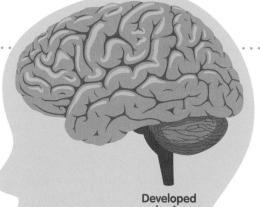

Developed brain

65,000 There are around 65,000 different species of vertebrate.

Vertebrates only make up around 3% of all the animals on Earth. The majority of animal species are invertebrates.

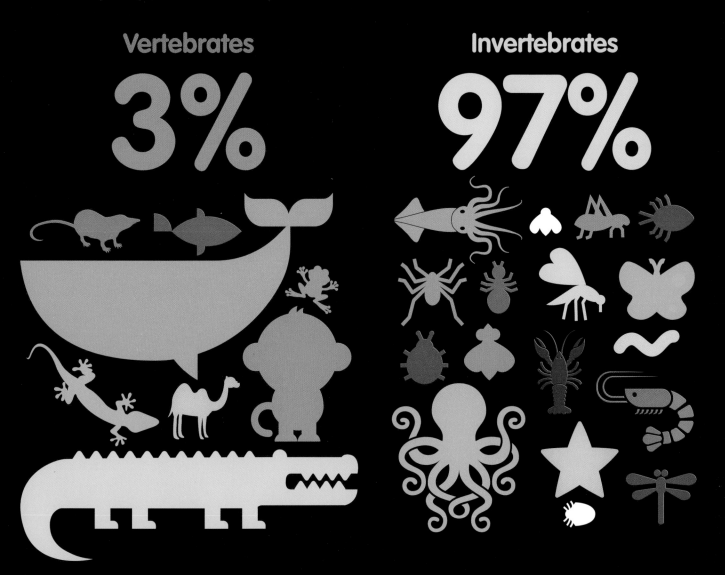

Vertebrates

3%

Invertebrates

97%

Invertebrates

Invertebrates are animals that do not have a backbone or an internal skeleton made of bone. Due to this, most invertebrates are small in size.

Invertebrates have other ways of supporting their bodies.

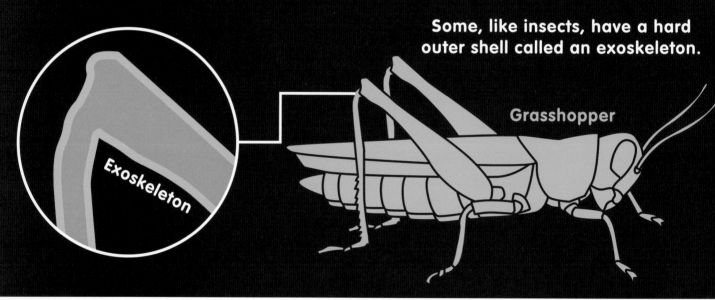

Some, like insects, have a hard outer shell called an exoskeleton.

Exoskeleton

Grasshopper

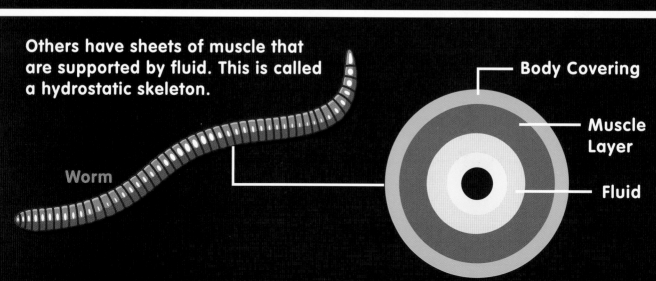

Others have sheets of muscle that are supported by fluid. This is called a hydrostatic skeleton.

Worm

Body Covering

Muscle Layer

Fluid

Arthropods are invertebrate animals that make up over 75% of the world's animal species. Most arthropods have a hard exoskeleton to protect them. Arthropods include insects, <u>crustaceans</u> and <u>arachnids</u>.

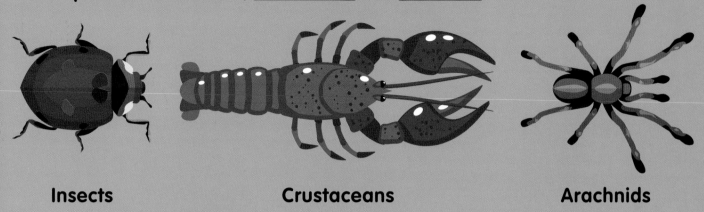

Insects   **Crustaceans**   **Arachnids**

Some species of invertebrates form colonies. This means that groups of animals stay together for most of their lives. They work together to keep the colony alive. Bees, ants and termites all live in colonies.

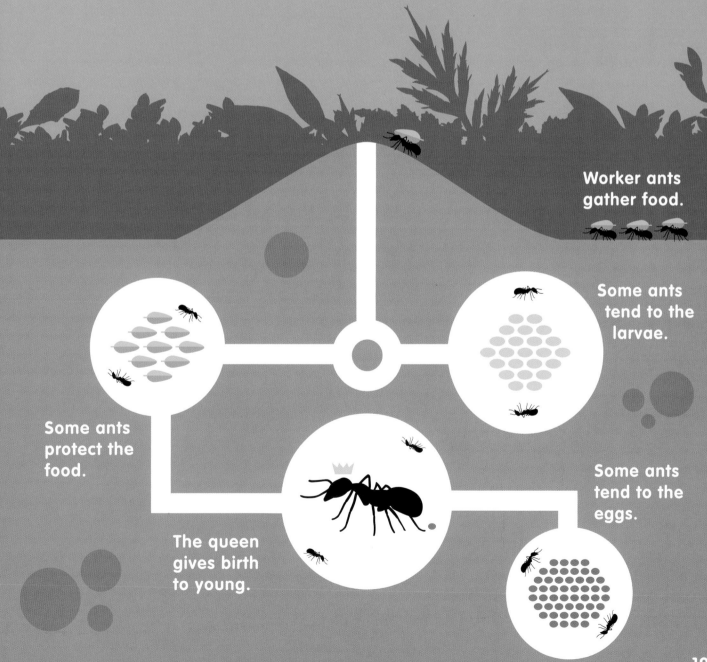

Worker ants gather food.

Some ants tend to the larvae.

Some ants protect the food.

Some ants tend to the eggs.

The queen gives birth to young.

Birth

Mammals grow inside their mothers' bodies until they are ready to be born. When they are big enough, the babies are born and feed on milk produced by their mothers.

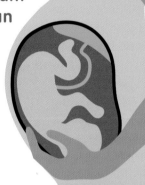

Kittens Feeding

Pregnant Woman

Reptiles and birds usually lay eggs. The babies grow inside the eggs until they are ready to hatch.

Bird's Eggs

Reptile Eggs

Amphibians and fish lay thousands or even millions of small, soft eggs in the water that hatch after varying amounts of time.

Fish Eggs

Once animals have been born, some stay with their parents for long periods of time while others become independent right away.

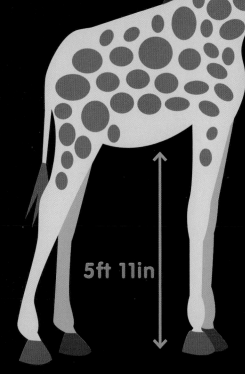

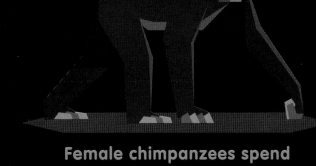

Female chimpanzees spend seven years raising their young.

5ft 11in

Giraffes give birth to their young standing up. This means that when the baby is born, it has a fall of 5ft 11in before it hits the ground!

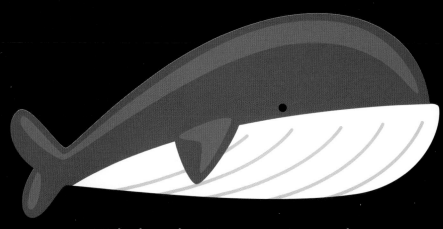

Whale calves consume around 120 gallons of their mother's milk every day.

Turtles lay their eggs on sand and leave immediately after.

An oyster produces millions of young in its lifetime.

Food and Growth

All animals need food to survive. Food gives animals the energy they need to help them to grow. Animals can be grouped based on the food they eat.

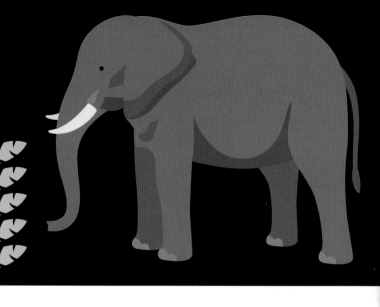

Carnivores: animals that feed on other animals.

Herbivores: animals that feed on plants.

Omnivores: animals that feed on other animals and plants.

Animals and plants are linked by food chains. Food chains show where each living organism gets the nutrients and energy that it requires to grow, move and stay alive. Every food chain starts with a plant, which is known as a producer.

Plants are called producers because they make their own food.

The rabbit eats the plant.

The hawk eats the rabbit.

Most animals and plants are part of more than one food chain.

An animal that eats another animal is called a predator.

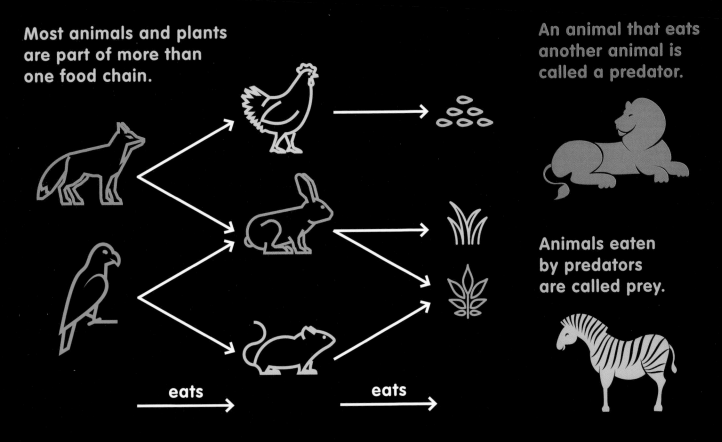

eats

eats

Animals eaten by predators are called prey.

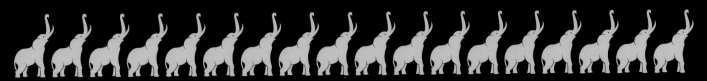

Adult elephants spend between 12 and 18 hours eating every day.

Reproduction

Reproduction is the process by which new organisms, or offspring, are produced. Every animal in the world exists because of reproduction.

Sexual

A male and female of the same species mate and produce offspring that receives a mixture of <u>genetic information</u> from both parents.

Offspring look similar to their parents, but not identical.

Most animals reproduce this way.

Asexual

Requires only one organism that produces a clone, or an exact copy, of itself.

There is no mixing of genetic information.

Most commonly found in plants, but some animals, such as starfish, also reproduce asexually.

The length of the **gestational period** varies greatly between animals.

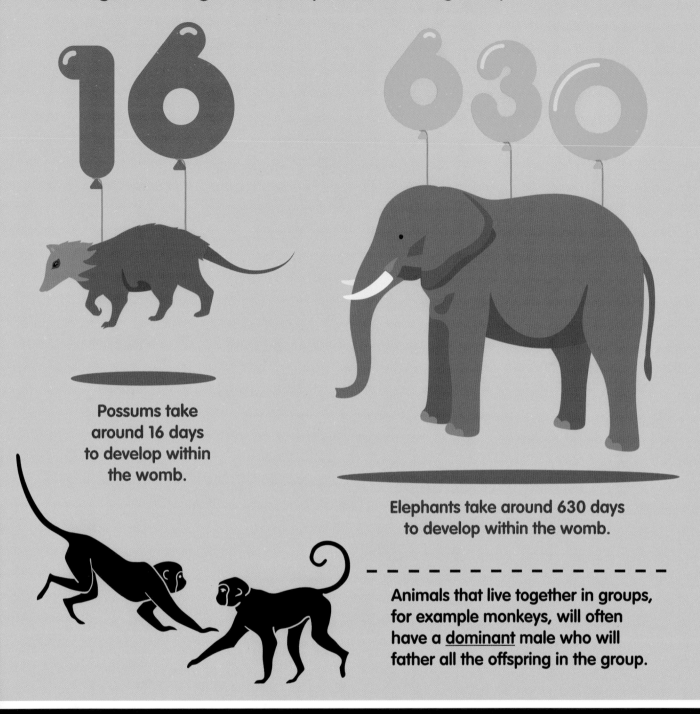

16

Possums take around 16 days to develop within the womb.

630

Elephants take around 630 days to develop within the womb.

- - - - - - - - - - - - - - - -

Animals that live together in groups, for example monkeys, will often have a **dominant** male who will father all the offspring in the group.

Dogs can experience false pregnancies. A female dog can experience pregnancy symptoms like vomiting even though they are not pregnant. They may even experience a false labor.

A female seahorse will lay her eggs inside the pouch of the male. The male will then take care of the eggs and give birth to the offspring!

Habitats

A habitat is the place, or environment, in which an animal lives. An ideal habitat provides an animal with food, water, shelter and a place to raise their young.

Ponds, woodlands and rainforests are all types of habitat.

A habitat can be very large or very small.

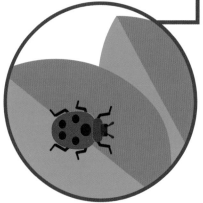

Small Habitat

Large Habitat

Habitats are constantly changing. During winter in the Arctic, the temperature is very low and much of the sea water around the Arctic freezes. In the summer, the temperature becomes warmer, large areas of ice melt away and the habitat size is greatly reduced.

Habitats all around the world are being destroyed. Forests are being cut down and rivers and lakes are being polluted. If a habitat is destroyed, the animals who lived there may have nowhere else to live.

Polluting Rivers   **Polluting Lakes**

Forest habitats are being destroyed all around the world.

Animals that live in the same habitat sometimes interact in order to help each other. Fruit bats disperse seeds from the fruit that they have eaten via their <u>excrement</u>, which helps to grow new plants for other animals to eat.

When a species of animal is at risk of becoming endangered, their habitat may become a "critical habitat." This means that the animals are protected by law so that they are not disturbed and can continue reproducing.

Adaptation

Adaptation is the process by which animals change over time so that their species is better suited to their habitat.

Many years ago, a man called Charles Darwin developed the theory of evolution through natural selection.

This means that animals that were best suited to an environment survived and those that weren't did not. When the animals that survived created offspring, they too had the traits that were more suited to their habitat.

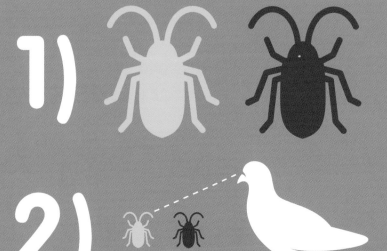

1) Some beetles are brown and some are green.

2) Green beetles are more easily seen by birds, and so are more likely to be eaten. The brown beetles survive, and go on to produce offspring.

3) The brown beetles have more opportunities to reproduce so there is a higher population of brown beetles.

Adaptations have happened in every species:

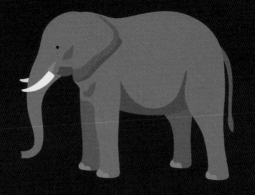

Frogs
Webbed feet
to swim faster

African Elephants
Big ears to fan
themselves in
the heat

Giraffes
Long necks so that
they can eat leaves
on higher trees

Not all features of an organism
will adapt over time and, as a result,
some animals are left with vestigial
structures or organs. These are features
that function normally in some species
but are no longer needed in others.

One example of vestigial structures are
the wings on non-flying birds, such as
the ostrich.

A species that is
poorly adapted to its
environment will be
at risk of extinction.

Activity

Draw your favorite animal

Look at the animal you have drawn and think about the ways in which it has adapted so that it is better suited to its habitat. Does it have sharp teeth for tearing food? Does it have a long neck to reach leaves in tall trees?

SHORT TAIL

CLAWS

Add labels to your drawing

Explain the different characteristics you have identified.

Improvements

How could the animal you have drawn be even better adapted to its habitat? Draw your animal again with any improvements you can think of.

ADDED SPIKES

Glossary

arachnids — a group of small animals with four pairs of legs, which includes spiders

blood vessels — tubes in the body through which blood flows

buoyancy — the ability of something to float

camouflage — to blend into surroundings so as not to be seen

cartilage — a type of strong tissue

crustaceans — animals that live in water and have a hard outer shell

dehydrate — to lose water

digits — fingers, thumbs or toes

dominant — the most important or strongest one

evolution — the way in which things change and develop over millions of years

excrement — poop is often called excrement

extinction — when a species has no living members

genetic information — information passed from parent to offspring via genes

gestational period — the period of development of a baby while still inside its mother's body

gills — the organs through which fish breathe

invertebrates — animals that do not have a backbone

organ — a part of the body that performs a particular function

organism — a living thing

protists — mold and some algae

replenish — fill something up again

reproduce — to produce young

tuatara — rare reptiles that are found in New Zealand

vertebrates — animals that have a backbone

Index

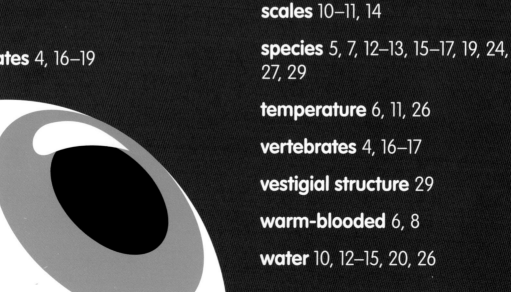